CREATE -A- SLEUTH

Writing a Detective Story

Written by Eleanor W. Hoomes, Ph.D
Cover Design by Nelsy Fontalvo

ACKNOWLEDGEMENTS

I wish to thank those special people—my students in the Heard County Enrichment Program in Heard County, Georgia, and my ex-students in the Carroll County Enrichment Program in Carroll County, Georgia—who have responded so beautifully when we have "done" creative writing. Without their responses, both positive and negative, I could never have arrived at a completed copy of *Create-a-Sleuth*.

Kathy Daniel Lipham has been a patient typist, working long and hard to help finish a final copy. Extra special thanks go to her.

And—my husband, Charles Wendell Hoomes, who finally said, "Either get it on paper and submit it to a publisher or hush," deserves some kind of thanks. Since I'm not sure what kind is due a tyrant, I'll simply say, "Thank you."

ISBN 0-910857-01-6

EDUCATIONAL IMPRESSIONS, INC.
Hawthorne, New Jersey 07507

Contents

Introduction to the Teacher

Students like to create, write and share stories; however, they can be baffled and become resentful when told to write a short story without being shown how to write one. Not knowing where nor how to begin, much less how to develop and end, they often write one skimpy paragraph and call it a short story. Conversely, when they are led through the structure of a story, step by step, they often surprise even themselves with the results.

Wise teachers capitalize on popular culture in the classroom. They begin with what is already familiar and interesting to students and use that knowledge and interest as springboards to introduce new knowledge. Building on the existing knowledge of and interest in detective fiction, the following teaching unit, *Create-a-Sleuth,* can be used as it is written, as a unit in creative writing, or it can be used as part of a unit on detective fiction. With a few modifications it can be used with grades four through twelve.

People of all ages are fascinated by those who are ''smarter'' than they are, and who intrigues the ''average'' person more than the ''smart'' detective who can solve a mystery with two grains of sand and one dog hair as the only clues? Edgar Allan Poe is credited with inventing the modern detective story, which he called the *ratiocinative tale.* Poe originated two devices widely used in detective stories. One is the baffled friend, who is not too bright (much like the reader) and who usually tells the story; the other device comes at the end of the story when the detective reveals the solution and then explains the step-by-step detection and deduction which led to that solution.

Interest in reading and viewing detective fiction starts at an early age. Students in elementary school start by reading Encyclopedia Brown stories and continue into adulthood with Father Brown stories. Students progress from the Hardy Boys and Nancy Drew to Jane Marple, Lord Peter Whimsey and Sherlock Holmes. The television detective show is a perennial favorite. Such past and current shows as *The Rockford Files, Hart to Hart, Magnum P.I., Columbo, Perry Mason, Father Dowling Mysteries,* and *Murder, She Wrote* attest to the drawing power of television detective shows.

Create-a-Sleuth will help develop students' abilities in observing, concluding, recalling, applying, analyzing, synthesizing, evaluating, and divergent and convergent thinking. At the same time it will contribute to the development of their oral, written and imaginative skills, with the additional advantage of being fun. And finally, it can give students an end product of which they will be proud.

The unit is designed to save thinking and preparation time for teachers and to encourage planned creativity. Some teachers neither need nor want minute descriptions of teaching approaches and objectives while other teachers, because of time limitations, need more detailed instructions. All are capable of modifying an idea to suit their own purposes and most prefer to innovate rather than copy. Therefore, teachers may use *Create-a-Sleuth* any way they wish, with only their imaginations limiting the various possibilities.

Teachers will readily see that *Create-a-Sleuth* may be used as a creative writing unit, or it can be used in conjunction with a literature unit on detective fiction. Either way, teachers using the unit will need to read aloud to students (or assign them to read) appropriate short detective fiction to generate interest and discussion.

Create-a-Sleuth is divided into two parts. The first part, composed of Activities 1 through 18, is sequential, building up to the writing of a detective story. Detailed teacher directions are given for each activity, with several options suggested for additional consideration. The second part, comprising Activities 19 through 22, simply offers additional choices. These last four activities may be used in many different ways, some of which are suggested in the teacher's directions at the beginning of the second section.

Behavioral objectives are not included as they are too precise and lengthy to include in a teaching unit of this type. No bibliography of suggested detective fiction is included because a quick trip to the library will yield sufficient information. Only a few examples of sleuths and detective fiction are included because teachers will need to vary their examples depending on the ages and abilities of their students.

I sincerely wish that *Create-a-Sleuth* will be as educational and as much fun for other teachers and students as it has been for my students and me.

Good luck!

Eleanor Wolfe Hoomes

NOTE: To increase the usefulness of this book, a duplicate set of student worksheet pages are provided. These perforated pages, which appear at the back of the book, may be detached for photocopying for use by the buyer in the classroom. This allows the teacher to keep the set of Teacher Directions and Student Pages side by side in the book.

Writing
a
Detective
Story

Definition of Sleuth

Objectives: To assist students in learning that many names may sometimes be used for the same thing (synonyms)

To help students understand that each synonym usually has a slight variation in meaning

To help students gain a working knowledge of *sleuth*

Thinking Skills: Observation

Recall

Application

Analysis

Introduction: Do you know what a sleuth is? (Most students will answer ''detective.'')

Do you know other names for *detective?*

What are the definitions of *sleuth* and *detective?*

What does a sleuth do?

In this unit on sleuths you will be analyzing the detectives you know, looking at what makes them interesting to read about or to watch on television or at the movies. You will also create your own sleuth and write your own detective story.

Directions: Discuss each synonym as to origin (or possible origin), use in detective fiction and variations in meaning. If other synonyms are given, work them into the discussion.

Options: Slang expressions and how they enter and become part of our language

Connotation and denotation

Formal and informal language

1993 Educational Impressions, Inc.

Definition of Sleuth

Activity No. 1

Student Work Sheet

A sleuth is a detective. A detective is one employed or engaged in catching lawbreakers or getting information that is not readily available. The word *sleuth* has many synonyms, one of which is *private investigator,* which is sometimes shortened to *P.I.* When the Pinkerton Detective Agency used an eye as part of its logo, the term *private eye* entered our language. How did each of the synonyms listed below come into use, and how does each vary in meaning?

Sleuth _____

_____

Detective _____

_____

Gumshoe _____

_____

Ferret _____

_____

Scout _____

_____

Spotter _____

_____

Mouser _____

_____

Pinkerton _____

_____

Dick _____

_____

Nose _____

_____

Bloodhound _____

_____

Famous Fictional Sleuths

Objectives: To encourage students to recall fictional sleuths

To promote student observation and analysis of distinctive personal characteristics and distinctive personality traits

Thinking Skills: Observation

Recall

Application

Analysis

Divergent Thinking

Introduction: Who is your favorite sleuth?

Is he/she a character in a book, comic book, comic strip, cartoon, television series or movie?

Why is he/she your favorite?

Directions: Discuss each name offered. Students will be more than willing to fill in gaps in the teacher's knowledge. Discuss the meaning of "distinguishing" characteristics. Fill in the first part of Activity No. 2 as a group, discussing each and reaching a consensus before moving on to the next. Students should fill in the bottom individually.

Options: The use of a major "quirk" to quickly establish a character

Authors of detective fiction/syndicates

Sleuths who appear in series of books (The Three Investigators, Encyclopedia Brown, Nancy Drew, Trixie Belden, the Hardy Boys)

Electronic and print media

1993 Educational Impressions, Inc.

Famous Fictional Sleuths

List famous fictional sleuths from books, comic books, TV, movies and comic strips in the left column. In the right column list at least one distinctive characteristic (more if you wish) of these sleuths.

Fictional Sleuth	**Distinguishing Characteristics**
1.	
2.	
3.	
4.	
5.	
6.	
7.	
8.	
9.	
10.	

What distinguishing characteristics might your sleuth possess?

_____

_____

_____

_____

Characteristics

Activity No. 3

Teacher Directions

Objectives: To assist students in understanding factors which make up the total person

To provoke students to question initial reactions to people based on superficial qualities

To guide students in selecting component parts of their sleuth

Thinking Skills: Recall

Application

Analysis

Synthesis

Evaluation

Introduction: What sex (race, age) is your favorite sleuth?

In what ways do sex (race, age) affect what your favorite sleuth does? How do they affect the way others respond to your favorite sleuth?

Directions: Discuss the effects of various characteristics of famous fictional sleuths. After students gain a thorough understanding of the effects, both positive and negative, of various characteristics, have them fill out Activity No. 3 individually. After the page is filled in, have students share their decisions and discuss the repercussions of each choice.

Options: Stereotypes

Female sleuths

Other minority sleuths

1993 Educational Impressions, Inc.

Characteristics

The sex, age, race, religion, dress, geographical origin, looks, and even the name of your sleuth determine how the public views him/her. These factors also help determine how the sleuth behaves. Think through what you want your sleuth to be or do before you determine each factor listed below.

Name _____

Sex _____

Age _____

Race _____

Religion _____

Geographical origin _____

Looks _____

   Height _____

   Weight _____

   Build _____

   Hair Color _____

   Eye Color _____

   Other _____

_____

_____

_____

Dress _____

_____

_____

_____

_____

Personality

Objectives: To assist students in examining and analyzing various types of personalities

To aid students in understanding how the personality of a sleuth determines to a large extent what he/she does in a story

To engage students in creating personalities for their sleuths

Thinking Skills: Recall

Understanding

Divergent thinking

Analysis

Synthesis

Introduction: What kind of personality does your favorite fictional sleuth have?

How does his/her personality contribute to the start, development and end of the story?

How does the personality of your favorite fictional sleuth cause others to react to him/her?

Directions: Discuss the above questions, making sure students understand the impact of the personality of a sleuth on a detective story. Return to Activity No. 2 and review quirks of famous fictional sleuths. Have students fill in Activity No. 4 individually and then have them share with the group.

Options: Outstanding personalities from literature

Outstanding present day personalities

Outstanding historical personalities

Personality

Some sleuths are intelligent and serious (Sherlock Holmes); some sleuths are stereotyped "middle-aged" women (Mrs. J.B. Fletcher) or "maiden" ladies (Miss Jane Marple); some sleuths are low key, pretending less intelligence than they actually have (Columbo); some sleuths are very "macho" (Thomas Magnum). What other types of sleuths can you think of? List them below.

Sleuth	Type
1. _____	_____
2. _____	_____
3. _____	_____
4. _____	_____
5. _____	_____

What kind of sleuth will yours be? You may use combinations from those listed above, or you may choose to be completely original and create a sleuth who does not fit an already created mold.

_____

_____

_____

_____

_____

Employment

Activity No. 5   **Teacher Directions**

Objectives: To guide students in analyzing the employment patterns of various fictional sleuths

To engage students in deciding the occupations of their created sleuths

To aid students in understanding that the chosen occupations of their sleuths have definite and continuous consequences

Thinking Skills: Recall

Application

Analysis

Divergent thinking

Synthesis

Introduction: What is the primary occupation of your favorite fictional sleuth?

How does that occupation serve to project your favorite sleuth into cases that need solving?

If your favorite fictional sleuth is not employed by a law enforcement agency, what is his/her relationship to law enforcement officers? How does that relationship serve to add tension to the story or to help resolve the story?

Directions: Discuss the above questions, using specific examples of fictional sleuths. Then have students fill in Activity No. 5 individually. Share and discuss students' decisions and their reasons for each decision.

Options: Public reaction to law enforcement officials

Fictional mavericks in law enforcement

Fictional sleuths who are mavericks in their chosen profession

                                      1993 Educational Impressions, Inc.

Employment

Sleuths may be connected with a law enforcement agency (Columbo, detectives on ''Law and Order''), or they may be private investigators (Nero Wolfe, Rockford). If the sleuths are members of law enforcement agencies, such as the FBI, highway patrol, sheriff's department or local or state police, or private investigators, they are paid for the services they perform. Instead of being employed and paid as detectives, sleuths may have jobs that catapult them into the midst of interesting mysteries (Quincy, medical examiner), or the sleuths may be private individuals who are constantly finding themselves in the midst of intrigue or trouble (the Harts, Nancy Drew). Sleuths who are not members of law enforcement agencies must have some sort of relationship with at least one law official, either helpful or adverse in nature. What will be the situation with your sleuth? Explain below.

_____

_____

_____

_____

_____

_____

_____

_____

_____

_____

_____

_____

_____

_____

_____

_____

Problems/Mysteries

Activity No. 6

Objectives: To promote an understanding that a sleuth must have a crisis, mystery or problem with which to deal; otherwise, there can be no story

To engage students in thinking about problems and how to solve them

To motivate students to create crisis situations which they will use later in creating their own stories

Thinking Skills: Recall

Application

Analysis

Divergent thinking

Convergent thinking

Introduction: What is a crisis?

What is a problem?

What is a mystery?

Are *crisis, problem,* and *mystery* the same? Why or why not?

What does *intervention* mean?

Directions: Discuss *mystery, problem* and *crisis* dealing with the variations in meaning and use in detective fiction. Discuss *intervention* and how intervention causes the story to happen. Have students fill in fictional sleuths and typical crisis situations in which they intervene. Discuss each. Then have students create their own crisis situations which they will use later. Share orally.

Options: Famous unsolved mysteries

Personal mysteries in which students have been involved

Natural mysteries

1993 Educational Impressions, Inc.

Problems/Mysteries

Activity No. 6

Without something to detect, sleuths would not exist. Sleuths need crisis situations or problems which require their intervention. Below list some fictional sleuths and the kinds of situations in which they typically intervene or some typical kinds of mysteries they solve.

Fictional Sleuths	**Situations**
1. _____	_____
2. _____	_____
3. _____	_____
4. _____	_____
5. _____	_____

What kinds of problems or mysteries would your sleuth be likely to solve?

1. _____

_____

2. _____

_____

3. _____

_____

4. _____

_____

5. _____

_____

Family

Objectives: To guide students in understanding the importance of family in the scheme of life

To impress on students that the roles played by various family members vary from family to family

To involve students in creating a family background for their sleuths

Thinking Skills: Recall

Application

Divergent thinking

Convergent thinking

Synthesis

Introduction: Do relatives play any part in the life of your favorite fictional sleuth?

If so, what parts do they play? Do they hinder, help, or are they just there?

Directions: Impress on students that family members may help, hinder or be indifferent to their created sleuths. In creating families for their sleuths, students may choose to omit some of the categories listed, or they may wish to emphasize some other relative—a cousin or an aunt, for instance. Have students fill in Activity No. 7 individually and then share with the group.

Options: Personal family relationships

Families today as compared to families of the past

The future of the family

Family

Sleuths have families. Sometimes certain members of the family play important parts in the lives of the sleuth (Nancy Drew's father). Sometimes family is mentioned, but not shown (Columbo's wife). Sometimes there is no mention of family. What kind of family does your sleuth have? What part do members of the family play in the sleuth's life?

Relatives' Names   Part Played

Parents

_____   _____

_____   _____

Siblings

_____   _____

_____   _____

_____   _____

Spouse

_____   _____

Children

_____   _____

_____   _____

Other Relatives

_____   _____

_____   _____

_____   _____

In-laws

_____   _____

_____   _____

_____   _____

Friendly Assistance

Activity No. 8

Objectives: To encourage students to examine relationships between people

To convey to students the importance of friendship

To guide students in the creation of friends and/or assistants for their created sleuths

Thinking Skills: Recall

Application

Analysis

Synthesis

Introduction: Does your favorite fictional sleuth have a close personal friend who helps him/her in solving cases? If so, what is the relationship like?

Does your favorite fictional sleuth have a paid assistant or is he/she a paid assistant? If so, what is the relationship between the superior and the subordinate?

Directions: Discuss relationships between famous fictional sleuths and their friends who also serve as assistants (Nancy Drew and George, Sherlock Holmes and Dr. Watson). Have students fill out Activity No. 8 individually and then share with the group.

Options: Personal friendships

Historical friendships

Fictional friendships

Friendly Assistance

Some sleuths receive assistance, either from paid helpers or from friends who help. These assistants also serve as sounding boards for the sleuth to explain how certain bits of detection is done. Create two characters who assist your sleuth in some way. If your sleuth is not connected with a law enforcement agency, you may wish to create one law official who assists your sleuth in some way.

Name _____

Age _____

Physical description _____
_____
_____

Distinguishing personality traits _____
_____
_____

Relationship to sleuth _____
_____

Name _____

Age _____

Physical description _____
_____
_____

Distinguishing personality traits _____
_____
_____

Relationship to sleuth _____
_____

Add others if you wish...

1993 Educational Impressions, Inc.

Animals

Activity No. 9

Teacher Directions

Objectives: To encourage students to examine relationships between animals and people

To aid students in understanding that people and animals differ and, therefore, relationships between animals and people differ

To engage students in creating animals and various roles for them

Thinking Skills: Recall

Application

Analysis

Synthesis

Divergent thinking

Convergent thinking

Introduction: Does your favorite fictional sleuth have a pet? If so, what are his/her feelings and actions toward the animal? How does the animal respond to its owner?

Does your favorite fictional sleuth have any superstition or irrational fears concerning animals? If so, what are they? Why, do you think, did the author include these in the character's make-up?

Directions: Discuss the above questions. Have students fill out the top half of Activity No. 9 individually and then discuss choices. Next have students fill out the bottom half in small groups. The brainstorming process could be used here. Share and encourage students to "spin-off" from each other's ideas.

Options: Animal intelligence and loyalty

Fictional animals that have been exceptional

Historical or legendary animals of importance

1993 Educational Impressions, Inc.

Animals

Activity No. 9

Some sleuths have a pet or animal which may or may not actually help in solving crimes. Create an animal for your sleuth. What will be its function in the story?

What is the animal? _____

What is its function? _____

_____

_____

What kinds of things does it do? _____

_____

_____

_____

_____

In addition, animals sometimes play important roles in mysteries. What roles might the following animals play in a mystery?

Snake _____

Spider _____

Horse _____

Goldfish _____

Elephant _____

Leopard _____

Canary _____

Porcupine _____

Skunk _____

Others _____

_____

Tools of the Trade

Activity No. 10

Objectives: To involve students in analyzing the uses of special tools, aliases and disguises in detective fiction

To assist students in projecting the outcome of ideas

To provide an opportunity for students to invent tools, aliases and disguises for their created sleuths

Thinking Skills: Recall

Analysis

Divergent thinking

Convergent thinking

Synthesis

Introduction: What special tools does your favorite fictional sleuth use? How does he/she use the tools?

Does your favorite fictional sleuth use aliases? If so, what are they? When and how are they used?

Does your favorite fictional sleuth use disguises? If so, what are they and why are they used? Do they work?

Directions: Discuss special tools, aliases and disguises used by various fictional sleuths. After establishing the various uses of each, have students fill out Activity No. 10. This can be done individually or in small groups. If small groups are used, brainstorming can be a useful device to generate multiple ideas. When all are finished, share.

Options: Disguises and aliases used by criminals

Equipment used by law enforcement agencies

Simple everyday materials which can be substituted for sophisticated hardware

1993 Educational Impressions, Inc.

Tools of the Trade

Sleuths often use special tools, disguises or aliases to help solve a mystery. What special tools will your sleuth need? How will he/she use the tools?

Tools	Uses
1. _____	_____
2. _____	_____
3. _____	_____
4. _____	_____

Will your sleuth use any special aliases? How?

Aliases	Purposes
1. _____	_____
2. _____	_____
3. _____	_____
4. _____	_____

Will your sleuth use any special disguises? Why?

Disguises	Reasons
1. _____	_____
2. _____	_____
3. _____	_____
4. _____	_____

Strengths

Objectives: To encourage students to examine various kinds of strengths—physical, mental and moral—and to make comparisons

To provoke students to look beneath the surface in order to find hidden strengths

To guide students in creating special abilities for their sleuths

Thinking Skills: Recall

Application

Analysis

Divergent thinking

Convergent thinking

Synthesis

Evaluation

Introduction: What special strengths does your favorite fictional sleuth possess?

Into what category do these strengths fall: physical, moral or mental?

Does he/she have special strengths in more than one category? Explain.

How do these special strengths help your favorite fictional sleuth in solving cases?

Directions: Arrive at a consensus of what a strength is. Next define physical strength, mental strength and moral strength. Add any other categories which fit. Direct students to fill out Activity No. 11 individually. Then have them share their final choices and the reasons for their choices.

Options: Famous "strong" men/women

Why people admire physical strength

Famous people of integrity

Strengths

Sleuths usually possess special strengths, either physical, mental or moral. What special strengths might your sleuth possess? How could these abilities contribute to the successes of your sleuth?

Strengths	**Contributions**
1. _____	_____
	_____
	_____
2. _____	_____
	_____
	_____
3. _____	_____
	_____
	_____
4. _____	_____
	_____
	_____
5. _____	_____
	_____
	_____

Now choose two special abilities from the list above that you would like your sleuth to possess. Be specific about how these special strengths will contribute to the success of your sleuth.

1. _____

_____

_____

2. _____

_____

Weaknesses

Activity No. 12

Teacher Directions

Objectives: To encourage students to examine various kinds of weaknesses—physical, mental and moral—and to make comparisons

To provoke students to look beneath the surface in order to find hidden weaknesses

To guide students in creating special weaknesses for their sleuths

Thinking Skills: Recall

Application

Analysis

Divergent thinking

Convergent thinking

Synthesis

Evaluation

Introduction: What special weaknesses does your favorite fictional sleuth possess?

Into what category do these weaknesses fall: physical, moral or mental?

Does he/she have special weaknesses in more than one category? Explain.

How do these special weaknesses hinder your favorite fictional sleuth in solving cases?

Directions: Arrive at a consensus of what a weakness is. Next define physical weakness, mental weakness and moral weakness. Add any other categories which fit. Direct students to fill out Activity No. 12 individually. Then have them share their final choices and the reasons for their choices.

Options: Personal feeling about own weaknesses

Fictional weak characters

Why people can accept some kinds of weaknesses and not others

1993 Educational Impressions, Inc.

Weaknesses

Sometimes sleuths will also have special weaknesses—either physical, mental or moral—which lead to complications. What special weaknesses might your sleuth possess? How might they contribute to the problems your sleuth faces?

Weaknesses	**Contributions**
1. _____	_____
	_____
	_____
2. _____	_____
	_____
	_____
3. _____	_____
	_____
	_____
4. _____	_____
	_____
	_____
5. _____	_____
	_____
	_____

Now choose two special weaknesses from the list above that your sleuth will possess. Be specific about how these special weaknesses will contribute to your sleuth's problems.

1. _____

_____

_____

2. _____

_____

_____

Values

Objectives:

To provide an atmosphere wherein students may openly examine and discuss values

To encourage students to reason and project the consequences of certain choices

To engage students in developing values for their sleuths

Thinking Skills:

Application

Analysis

Divergent thinking

Convergent thinking

Synthesis

Evaluation

Introduction:

What are some of the values held by your favorite fictional sleuth? Do you consider those values to be worthwhile? Explain.

Do the values held by your favorite fictional sleuth help or hinder him/her in the solving of a case? How do they affect the decisions made by the sleuth?

Directions:

Arrive at a working definition of *values*. Guide students in understanding that what people value determines the decisions they make and the actions they take. Discuss the questions in the Introduction. Have students fill out Activity No. 13 individually. Share the highest ranked values and the projected consequences of holding those values.

Options:

Decision making

How peers affect students' values

How culture helps determine values

1993 Educational Impressions, Inc.

Values

Sleuths hold certain values. A sleuth may value honesty or loyalty or promptness. List ten or more values your sleuth will consider important. Rank these on a scale of 1 to 10, 10 being the most important value; 1 being the least important value.

Value	Rank
1.	
2.	
3.	
4.	
5.	
7.	
8.	
9.	
10.	

Look at the four highest ranked values. How will the valuing of these qualities affect the behavior of your sleuth?

1. _____

_____

2. _____

_____

3. _____

_____

4. _____

_____

Villains

Objectives: To guide students in understanding the importance of conflict in a story

To assist students in analyzing various kinds of conflict

To involve students in creating possible villains for their sleuths

Thinking Skills: Recall

Analysis

Divergent thinking

Convergent thinking

Synthesis

Evaluation

Introduction: Who are some of the villains your favorite fictional sleuth faces? Does he/she have new and different ones for each story, or does he/she face the same one(s) over and over?

What could be the advantage of using the same villain again?

Directions: Make sure that students understand that a well drawn villain is just as important as a well designed sleuth. The villain(s) must always be worthy of the sleuth. Have students create four possible villains. Then have them pick their best one. Tell them to hold the others for possible use later.

Options: Conflict

Famous fictional villains

Infamous historical villains

1993 Educational Impressions, Inc.

Villains

Some sleuths face the same opponent(s), also called enemies, archenemies, foes, or villains, over and over (Sherlock Holmes *vs.* Professor Moriarty). Others face their opponents only once. List below four possible opponents for your sleuth. Give the villain's name, profession or occupation, some distinguishing physical and character traits, strengths and weaknesses. What does the villain value most and why?

1. _____

_____

_____

2. _____

_____

_____

3. _____

_____

_____

4. _____

_____

_____

Now go back and pick one villain who will be the major enemy of your sleuth. Why did you choose the one you chose?

Villain_____

_____

Reason _____

_____

_____

Origin

Activity No. 15

Objectives: To encourage students to think about how something begins

To assist students in reasoning the possible future developments because of various kinds of beginnings

To provide an atmosphere wherein students may create origins for their sleuths

Thinking Skills: Recall

Analysis

Divergent thinking

Convergent thinking

Synthesis

Evaluation

Introduction: How did your favorite fictional sleuth get his/her start in the detecting business?

How important to later developments was the origin of your favorite fictional sleuth?

Directions: Make sure that students understand the words *origin* and *beginning*. Help them be selective in the point where they actually start their sleuths. Fill out Activity No. 15 individually. Check to make sure students have been consistent in the details of their sleuth's origins.

Options: The Bible (''In the beginning...'')

Fairy tales (''Once upon a time...'')

''Roots''

Origin

Sleuths must begin somewhere and somehow. Why and how did your sleuth get into the detecting business? What happened or who influenced your sleuth to start sleuthing?

When? _____

_____

_____

Where? _____

_____

_____

Why? _____

_____

_____

How? _____

_____

_____

Who? _____

_____

_____

What? _____

_____

_____

Keeping Records

Activity No. 16

Teacher Directions

Objectives: To aid students in thinking about the common activities which are necessary while living through a day

To assist students in selection and condensation

To involve students in creating a typical day for their sleuths

Thinking Skills: Recall

Analysis

Synthesis

Evaluation

Introduction: What would a typical day be like for your favorite fictional sleuth? Would every minute be composed of exciting adventure? Would there be time to do ordinary, necessary things? For instance, who makes the bed, does the laundry, cooks the meals and does the shopping?

Directions: Guide students through a typical day verbally. They might use their own day. Start at the beginning and go to the end. Then assist students in selecting and condensing for conciseness and interest. Next have them do Activity No. 16 in which they create a typical day for their sleuths. Finally, lead them through the selection and condensation process again.

Options: Famous journals

Personal journals

1993 Educational Impressions, Inc.

Keeping Records

While record keeping is not encountered in the majority of detective fiction, it is used in some. When it is used, the stories are written in diary (or log or journal) style with date, time and terse statements of actions, reactions, feeling suppositions and other tidbits of information. Create a typical day for your sleuth, including common, ordinary details, such as food eaten. Use enough of this information when you get to Activity No. 18 to make your story believable, but not so much that you overburden your story with minutia.

_____

_____

_____

_____

_____

_____

_____

_____

_____

_____

_____

_____

_____

_____

_____

_____

_____

_____

_____

Clues

Objectives: To assist students in understanding the importance of clues in solving mysteries

To assist students in analyzing various methods of using clues

To engage students in creating clues for their sleuths to use

Thinking Skills: Recall

Analysis

Divergent Thinking

Synthesis

Evaluation

Introduction: What are some of the unusual clues your favorite sleuth has encountered? Did he/she recognize their importance at first? Did he/she ever use a combination of clues to solve a case? If so, what were they and how and why did he/she combine them?

Directions: Discuss the use of clues in solving mysteries. Help students to be logical and consistent in the use of clues when they create their own. Have students share orally to see if their reasoning is valid.

Options: Discuss "red herrings." *Red herring,* a term meaning *camouflage,* comes from a process of curing herring. When a herring is salted and smoked slowly over a wood fire, it turns a dark reddish brown color and gains a strong flavor and scent. The smell is so strong that it overwhelms other scents. According to some old tales, red herrings were pulled across the trail of hounds to confuse and throw them off the trail. Sometimes writers of detective fiction deliberately mislead readers by planting misleading clues, known as red herrings.

Riddles

Clues

How do sleuths solve their cases? With clues, of course. Clues take many forms. They may be footprints, hairs, tire tracks or fibers. Don't forget the old standards, the fingerprint and the lipprint! For younger sleuths, secret codes, puzzles and riddles are often important clues. Below list some clues that might be used by your sleuth in solving a mystery. Will any of your clues be red herrings?

Clues	**Importance**
1. _____	_____
2. _____	_____
3. _____	_____
4. _____	_____
5. _____	_____
6. _____	_____
7. _____	_____
8. _____	_____
9. _____	_____
10. _____	_____

Clues are also used in combination to "crack a case." How could you combine some of the clues you listed above?

_____

_____

_____

_____

_____

_____

_____

Writing the Story

Activity No. 18

Teacher Directions

Objectives: To assist students in choosing the tense and person to be used in writing their stories

To aid students in the construction of a short story

To engage students in writing a short story

Thinking Skills: Analysis

Synthesis

Evaluation

Introduction: Point of view is important in a story. Will you use first person point of view, where ''I'' is used and details are filtered through the eyes of the person telling the story? Will you use third person limited point of view, where ''he'' or ''she'' is used and all details are filtered through the eyes of the main ''he'' or ''she''? Will you use third person omniscient point of view, where ''he,'' ''she'' and ''they'' are all revealed to the reader without being filtered through one main character? What will be the advantages and limitations of each?

In what tense will you write your story? Why?

Directions: Discuss point of view, tense and the construction of a short story. Then have students write their stories, using the materials created in Activities 2 through 17.

Options: Activities 19 through 22

Writing the Story

Based upon all the information which you have compiled on your sleuth, write a short story detailing how your sleuth got into the sleuthing business. Treat this short story as the first in a series of exciting adventures. Remember to use direct conversation and direct action. Also remember that a short story occurs in three parts:

1. the **beginning**, where the characters and situation(s) are introduced,

2. the **middle**, where complication arise (a series of complications or problems may be encountered here), and

3. the **ending**, where the complications are resolved.

There are certain standards which a ''good'' detective story should meet. Before you write your story, study the following **rules for detective fiction.**

1. The reader should learn of evidence and clues as the detective learns about them. The reader should share in the discoveries as they are made.

2. The villain should be a fairly important character in the story.

3. The villain should have a motive that is understandable to the reader.

4. Generally, crime should not be accidental. However, the original misbehavior can be accidental if subsequent behavior to cover it up is criminal or leads to criminal behavior.

5. Generally, a death under investigation should not be suicide.

6. The story should not contain supernatural occurrences or other happenings which cannot be rationally explained.

If you intend to use your villain again, you must leave him/her alive at the end, in a situation which temporarily resolves the complications, but which leaves him/her capable of further mischief.

Additional Options

Activities 19 through 22   **Teacher Directions**

Objectives: To provide opportunities for those students who wish to continue writing detective fiction

Thinking Skills: Recall

Observation

Application

Analysis

Divergent thinking

Convergent thinking

Synthesis

Evaluation

Directions: Activities 19 through 22 can be used to extend the *Create-a-Sleuth* unit, as follow-ups at later dates during the year, before beginning Activity No. 1, or individually as one-shot writing assignments. No individual teacher directions are given; instead, the student pages are fairly complete within themselves.

Other Ways to Use a Sleuth

Activity No. 19

Student Work Sheet

In addition to writing a short story using your created sleuth, you may wish to try some of the following suggestions:

1. Write a radio script. With appropriate sound effects, the script may be produced for an audience by simply using a screen to conceal the participants from their audience. The script could also be recorded on a tape recorder and then played for the audience. Don't overlook the use of music to achieve startling effects.

2. Write a play. A play is not complete unless it is staged. Producing a play involves more work than producing a radio show because the audience sees the actors. Lines and actions must be learned; whereas, in a radio show, the lines can be read. If you have access to a movie camera or a video-sound system, filming the play could be an interesting experience.

3. Draw a comic strip. Study a comic book first so that you are thoroughly familiar with all the conventions of comic book writing.

4. Write a narrative poem. Treat your sleuth as either an epic hero/heroine or a comic hero/heroine.

5. Write a song. Set it to music and record it on a tape recorder.

6. Draw a filmstrip of the story you wrote in Activity No. 18 or write a new story. Record the story on a tape recorder and synchronize the two to show to an audience.

7. Draw a cartoon of your created sleuth in a situation which reveals his/her true personality and character.

Locked Room Mysteries

Locked room mysteries are a staple of detective fiction. Edgar Allan Poe is credited with writing the first detective story, which was a locked room mystery. In the 150 years since Poe wrote ''Murders in the Rue Morgue,'' thousands more have been written. One of the better known locked room mysteries is Arthur Conan Doyle's ''The Adventures of the Speckled Band.'' A more recent anthology of locked room mysteries is entitled *Tantalizing Locked Room Mysteries,* edited by Isaac Asimov, Charles G. Waugh and Martin Harry Greenberg.

Using the sleuth you have already created, write a locked room mystery. Be thorough in planning the mystery; work out how it will begin, develop and end before you start writing.

Sketch in the space below the room and how it relates to the rest of the building and the surrounding grounds. Work out the details so that the whole puzzle is put together smoothly in the end.

Group Created Stories

Using the basic material in Activities 2 through 18, create group stories using the following process:

Divide into groups of four students.

Each select a different one of the following tasks:

1. Create a sleuth
2. Create a villain
3. Create a setting and three clues
4. Create a situation, a crisis and complications

After you have completed the above assignment individually, return to your group. Now put your imagination to work, using the materials you have created to write one of the following (see Activity No. 19):

1. A short story
2. A radio script
3. A play
4. A poem
5. A song
6. A comic strip
7. A filmstrip

Story Starters

You may wish to use the following sleuths in a short story or in one of the ways suggested in Activity No. 19.

Bob (Charles Robert) and Betty (Elizabeth Janine) Boatwright are fourteen-year-old twins. Bob is a slow, concrete, logical thinker; Betty is a quick, intuitive, creative thinker. They are both enrolled in special classes for gifted students. They have a two-year-old female German shepherd named Nosey. Their father, Dr. Charles Boatwright, is Chairman of the Criminal Justice Department at Chandler College. Their mother, Dr. Catherine Boatwright, is Professor of Psychology at the same college. An uncle, Jack Harris, young and handsome bachelor brother of Catherine, is Chief of Police at Chandlerville. Chandlerville has a population of about 12,000. Since Betty and Bob are fourteen, their only modes of transport are bicycles, horses, hitchhiking (frowned on by their parents), public transportation, or being driven by their parents or other adults. Both Bob and Betty have short, curly auburn hair. Bob can disguise as a girl. Betty can disguise as a boy and sometimes as an older girl.

Story Starters:

1. Bob and Betty are the first students to arrive at school. As they start to enter the building, they hear a mysterious noise coming from inside. They quickly push the door open and are amazed at what they see.

2. Bob and Betty are taking Nosey for a walk in the country one beautiful spring afternoon. As they pass Miss Hazel's house, Miss Hazel bursts through her front door, yelling, "Help! I've been robbed! Help!"

3. Bob answers the telephone. In a muffled voice, a stranger says, "I have your dog Nosey. She will be returned to you safe and sound only if you do as I say..."

4. Write your own story starters and swap with a classmate.

Tear-out Reproducible Student Work Pages

Definition of Sleuth

A sleuth is a detective. A detective is one employed or engaged in catching lawbreakers or getting information that is not readily available. The word *sleuth* has many synonyms, one of which is *private investigator,* which is sometimes shortened to *P.I.* When the Pinkerton Detective Agency used an eye as part of its logo, the term *private eye* entered our language. How did each of the synonyms listed below come into use, and how does each vary in meaning?

Sleuth _____

_____

Detective _____

_____

Gumshoe _____

_____

Ferret _____

_____

Scout _____

_____

Spotter _____

_____

Mouser _____

_____

Pinkerton _____

_____

Dick _____

_____

Nose _____

_____

Bloodhound _____

_____

Famous Fictional Sleuths

Activity No. 2   **Student Work Sheet**

List famous fictional sleuths from books, comic books, TV, movies and comic strips in the left column. In the right column list at least one distinctive characteristic (more if you wish) of these sleuths.

Fictional Sleuth	Distinguishing Characteristics
1. _____	_____
2. _____	_____
3. _____	_____
4. _____	_____
5. _____	_____
6. _____	_____
7. _____	_____
8. _____	_____
9. _____	_____
10. _____	_____

What distinguishing characteristics might your sleuth possess?

_____

_____

_____

_____

                                    1993 Educational Impressions, Inc.

Characteristics

Activity No. 3   **Student Work Sheet**

The sex, age, race, religion, dress, geographical origin, looks, and even the name of your sleuth determine how the public views him/her. These factors also help determine how the sleuth behaves. Think through what you want your sleuth to be or do before you determine each factor listed below.

Name _____

Sex _____

Age _____

Race _____

Religion _____

Geographical origin _____

Looks _____

   Height _____

   Weight_____

   Build _____

   Hair Color _____

   Eye Color _____

   Other _____

     _____

     _____

     _____

Dress _____

_____

_____

_____

_____

Personality

Some sleuths are intelligent and serious (Sherlock Holmes); some sleuths are stereotyped "middle-aged" women (Mrs. J.B. Fletcher) or "maiden" ladies (Miss Jane Marple); some sleuths are low key, pretending less intelligence than they actually have (Columbo); some sleuths are very "macho" (Thomas Magnum). What other types of sleuths can you think of? List them below.

	Sleuth	**Type**
1.	_____	_____
2.	_____	_____
3.	_____	_____
4.	_____	_____
5.	_____	_____

What kind of sleuth will yours be? You may use combinations from those listed above, or you may choose to be completely original and create a sleuth who does not fit an already created mold.

_____

_____

_____

_____

_____

Employment

Sleuths may be connected with a law enforcement agency (Columbo, detectives on "Law and Order"), or they may be private investigators (Nero Wolfe, Rockford). If the sleuths are members of law enforcement agencies, such as the FBI, highway patrol, sheriff's department or local or state police, or private investigators, they are paid for the services they perform. Instead of being employed and paid as detectives, sleuths may have jobs that catapult them into the midst of interesting mysteries (Quincy, medical examiner), or the sleuths may be private individuals who are constantly finding themselves in the midst of intrigue or trouble (the Harts, Nancy Drew). Sleuths who are not members of law enforcement agencies must have some sort of relationship with at least one law official, either helpful or adverse in nature. What will be the situation with your sleuth? Explain below.

_____

_____

_____

_____

_____

_____

_____

_____

_____

_____

_____

_____

_____

_____

_____

_____

Problems/Mysteries

Without something to detect, sleuths would not exist. Sleuths need crisis situations or problems which require their intervention. Below list some fictional sleuths and the kinds of situations in which they typically intervene or some typical kinds of mysteries they solve.

Fictional Sleuths	**Situations**
1. _____	_____
2. _____	_____
3. _____	_____
4. _____	_____
5. _____	_____

What kinds of problems or mysteries would your sleuth be likely to solve?

1. _____

_____

2. _____

_____

3. _____

_____

4. _____

_____

5. _____

_____

1993 Educational Impressions, Inc.

Family

Sleuths have families. Sometimes certain members of the family play important parts in the lives of the sleuth (Nancy Drew's father). Sometimes family is mentioned, but not shown (Columbo's wife). Sometimes there is no mention of family. What kind of family does your sleuth have? What part do members of the family play in the sleuth's life?

Relatives' Names	**Part Played**
Parents	
_____	_____
_____	_____
Siblings	
_____	_____
_____	_____
_____	_____
Spouse	
_____	_____
Children	
_____	_____
_____	_____
_____	_____
Other Relatives	
_____	_____
_____	_____
_____	_____
In-laws	
_____	_____
_____	_____
_____	_____

Friendly Assistance

Some sleuths receive assistance, either from paid helpers or from friends who help. These assistants also serve as sounding boards for the sleuth to explain how certain bits of detection is done. Create two characters who assist your sleuth in some way. If your sleuth is not connected with a law enforcement agency, you may wish to create one law official who assists your sleuth in some way.

Name _____

Age _____

Physical description _____

_____

_____

Distinguishing personality traits _____

_____

_____

Relationship to sleuth _____

_____

Name _____

Age _____

Physical description _____

_____

_____

Distinguishing personality traits _____

_____

_____

Relationship to sleuth _____

_____

Add others if you wish...

Animals

Some sleuths have a pet or animal which may or may not actually help in solving crimes. Create an animal for your sleuth. What will be its function in the story?

What is the animal? _____

What is its function? _____

_____

_____

What kinds of things does it do? _____

_____

_____

_____

_____

In addition, animals sometimes play important roles in mysteries. What roles might the following animals play in a mystery?

Snake _____

Spider _____

Horse _____

Goldfish _____

Elephant _____

Leopard _____

Canary _____

Porcupine _____

Skunk _____

Others _____

_____

Tools of the Trade

Sleuths often use special tools, disguises or aliases to help solve a mystery. What special tools will your sleuth need? How will he/she use the tools?

Tools	Uses
1. _____	_____
2. _____	_____
3. _____	_____
4. _____	_____

Will your sleuth use any special aliases? How?

Aliases	Purposes
1. _____	_____
2. _____	_____
3. _____	_____
4. _____	_____

Will your sleuth use any special disguises? Why?

Disguises	Reasons
1. _____	_____
2. _____	_____
3. _____	_____
4. _____	_____

Strengths

Sleuths usually possess special strengths, either physical, mental or moral. What special strengths might your sleuth possess? How could these abilities contribute to the successes of your sleuth?

Strengths	**Contributions**
1. _____	_____
	_____
	_____
2. _____	_____
	_____
	_____
3. _____	_____
	_____
	_____
4. _____	_____
	_____
	_____
5. _____	_____
	_____
	_____

Now choose two special abilities from the list above that you would like your sleuth to possess. Be specific about how these special strengths will contribute to the success of your sleuth.

1. _____

_____

_____

2. _____

_____

_____

Weaknesses

Sometimes sleuths will also have special weaknesses—either physical, mental or moral—which lead to complications. What special weaknesses might your sleuth possess? How might they contribute to the problems your sleuth faces?

Weaknesses	**Contributions**
1. _____	_____
	_____
	_____
2. _____	_____
	_____
	_____
3. _____	_____
	_____
	_____
4. _____	_____
	_____
	_____
5. _____	_____
	_____
	_____

Now choose two special weaknesses from the list above that your sleuth will possess. Be specific about how these special weaknesses will contribute to your sleuth's problems.

1. _____

_____

_____

2. _____

_____

_____

1993 Educational Impressions, Inc.

Values

Activity No. 13   **Student Work Sheet**

Sleuths hold certain values. A sleuth may value honesty or loyalty or promptness. List ten or more values your sleuth will consider important. Rank these on a scale of 1 to 10, 10 being the most important value; 1 being the least important value.

Value   **Rank**

1. _____   _____

2. _____   _____

3. _____   _____

4. _____   _____

5. _____   _____

7. _____   _____

8. _____   _____

9. _____   _____

10. _____

Look at the four highest ranked values. How will the valuing of these qualities affect the behavior of your sleuth?

1. _____

_____

2. _____

_____

3. _____

_____

4. _____

_____

Villains

Some sleuths face the same opponent(s), also called enemies, archenemies, foes, or villains, over and over (Sherlock Holmes *vs.* Professor Moriarty). Others face their opponents only once. List below four possible opponents for your sleuth. Give the villain's name, profession or occupation, some distinguishing physical and character traits, strengths and weaknesses. What does the villain value most and why?

1. _____

_____

_____

2. _____

_____

_____

3. _____

_____

_____

4. _____

_____

_____

Now go back and pick one villain who will be the major enemy of your sleuth. Why did you choose the one you chose?

Villain_____

_____

Reason _____

_____

_____

1993 Educational Impressions, Inc.

Origin

Activity No. 15

Student Work Sheet

Sleuths must begin somewhere and somehow. Why and how did your sleuth get into the detecting business? What happened or who influenced your sleuth to start sleuthing?

When? _____

_____

_____

Where? _____

_____

_____

Why? _____

_____

_____

How? _____

_____

_____

Who? _____

_____

_____

What? _____

_____

_____

Keeping Records

While record keeping is not encountered in the majority of detective fiction, it is used in some. When it is used, the stories are written in diary (or log or journal) style with date, time and terse statements of actions, reactions, feeling suppositions and other tidbits of information. Create a typical day for your sleuth, including common, ordinary details, such as food eaten. Use enough of this information when you get to Activity No. 18 to make your story believable, but not so much that you overburden your story with minutia.

_____

_____

_____

_____

_____

_____

_____

_____

_____

_____

_____

_____

_____

_____

_____

_____

_____

1993 Educational Impressions, Inc.

Clues

How do sleuths solve their cases? With clues, of course. Clues take many forms. They may be footprints, hairs, tire tracks or fibers. Don't forget the old standards, the fingerprint and the lipprint! For younger sleuths, secret codes, puzzles and riddles are often important clues. Below list some clues that might be used by your sleuth in solving a mystery. Will any of your clues be red herrings?

	Clues	**Importance**
1.	_____	_____
2.	_____	_____
3.	_____	_____
4.	_____	_____
5.	_____	_____
6.	_____	_____
7.	_____	_____
8.	_____	_____
9.	_____	_____
10.	_____	_____

Clues are also used in combination to "crack a case." How could you combine some of the clues you listed above?

_____

_____

_____

_____

_____

_____

_____

Writing the Story

Based upon all the information which you have compiled on your sleuth, write a short story detailing how your sleuth got into the sleuthing business. Treat this short story as the first in a series of exciting adventures. Remember to use direct conversation and direct action. Also remember that a short story occurs in three parts:

1. the **beginning**, where the characters and situation(s) are introduced,

2. the **middle**, where complication arise (a series of complications or problems may be encountered here), and

3. the **ending**, where the complications are resolved.

There are certain standards which a ''good'' detective story should meet. Before you write your story, study the following **rules for detective fiction.**

1. The reader should learn of evidence and clues as the detective learns about them. The reader should share in the discoveries as they are made.

2. The villain should be a fairly important character in the story.

3. The villain should have a motive that is understandable to the reader.

4. Generally, crime should not be accidental. However, the original misbehavior can be accidental if subsequent behavior to cover it up is criminal or leads to criminal behavior.

5. Generally, a death under investigation should not be suicide.

6. The story should not contain supernatural occurrences or other happenings which cannot be rationally explained.

If you intend to use your villain again, you must leave him/her alive at the end, in a situation which temporarily resolves the complications, but which leaves him/her capable of further mischief.

Other Ways to Use a Sleuth

Activity No. 19

Student Work Sheet

In addition to writing a short story using your created sleuth, you may wish to try some of the following suggestions:

1. Write a radio script. With appropriate sound effects, the script may be produced for an audience by simply using a screen to conceal the participants from their audience. The script could also be recorded on a tape recorder and then played for the audience. Don't overlook the use of music to achieve startling effects.

2. Write a play. A play is not complete unless it is staged. Producing a play involves more work than producing a radio show because the audience sees the actors. Lines and actions must be learned; whereas, in a radio show, the lines can be read. If you have access to a movie camera or a video-sound system, filming the play could be an interesting experience.

3. Draw a comic strip. Study a comic book first so that you are thoroughly familiar with all the conventions of comic book writing.

4. Write a narrative poem. Treat your sleuth as either an epic hero/heroine or a comic hero/heroine.

5. Write a song. Set it to music and record it on a tape recorder.

6. Draw a filmstrip of the story you wrote in Activity No. 18 or write a new story. Record the story on a tape recorder and synchronize the two to show to an audience.

7. Draw a cartoon of your created sleuth in a situation which reveals his/her true personality and character.

Locked Room Mysteries

Locked room mysteries are a staple of detective fiction. Edgar Allan Poe is credited with writing the first detective story, which was a locked room mystery. In the 150 years since Poe wrote "Murders in the Rue Morgue," thousands more have been written. One of the better known locked room mysteries is Arthur Conan Doyle's "The Adventures of the Speckled Band." A more recent anthology of locked room mysteries is entitled *Tantalizing Locked Room Mysteries,* edited by Isaac Asimov, Charles G. Waugh and Martin Harry Greenberg.

Using the sleuth you have already created, write a locked room mystery. Be thorough in planning the mystery; work out how it will begin, develop and end before you start writing.

Sketch in the space below the room and how it relates to the rest of the building and the surrounding grounds. Work out the details so that the whole puzzle is put together smoothly in the end.

1993 Educational Impressions, Inc.

Group Created Stories

Activity No. 21

Using the basic material in Activities 2 through 18, create group stories using the following process:

Divide into groups of four students.

Each select a different one of the following tasks:

1. Create a sleuth

2. Create a villain

3. Create a setting and three clues

4. Create a situation, a crisis and complications

After you have completed the above assignment individually, return to your group. Now put your imagination to work, using the materials you have created to write one of the following (see Activity No. 19):

1. A short story

2. A radio script

3. A play

4. A poem

5. A song

6. A comic strip

7. A filmstrip

Story Starters

You may wish to use the following sleuths in a short story or in one of the ways suggested in Activity No. 19.

Bob (Charles Robert) and Betty (Elizabeth Janine) Boatwright are fourteen-year-old twins. Bob is a slow, concrete, logical thinker; Betty is a quick, intuitive, creative thinker. They are both enrolled in special classes for gifted students. They have a two-year-old female German shepherd named Nosey. Their father, Dr. Charles Boatwright, is Chairman of the Criminal Justice Department at Chandler College. Their mother, Dr. Catherine Boatwright, is Professor of Psychology at the same college. An uncle, Jack Harris, young and handsome bachelor brother of Catherine, is Chief of Police at Chandlerville. Chandlerville has a population of about 12,000. Since Betty and Bob are fourteen, their only modes of transport are bicycles, horses, hitchhiking (frowned on by their parents), public transportation, or being driven by their parents or other adults. Both Bob and Betty have short, curly auburn hair. Bob can disguise as a girl. Betty can disguise as a boy and sometimes as an older girl.

Story Starters:

1. Bob and Betty are the first students to arrive at school. As they start to enter the building, they hear a mysterious noise coming from inside. They quickly push the door open and are amazed at what they see.

2. Bob and Betty are taking Nosey for a walk in the country one beautiful spring afternoon. As they pass Miss Hazel's house, Miss Hazel bursts through her front door, yelling, "Help! I've been robbed! Help!"

3. Bob answers the telephone. In a muffled voice, a stranger says, "I have your dog Nosey. She will be returned to you safe and sound only if you do as I say..."

4. Write your own story starters and swap with a classmate.